T0271054

CAMBRIDGE LIBRARY COLLECTION

Books of enduring scholarly value

History

The books reissued in this series include accounts of historical events and movements by eye-witnesses and contemporaries, as well as landmark studies that assembled significant source materials or developed new historiographical methods. The series includes work in social, political and military history on a wide range of periods and regions, giving modern scholars ready access to influential publications of the past.

My African Travels

Published in 1886, My African Travels is a succinct record of British American explorer Henry Morton Stanley's adventurous African expeditions during 1871-1884 and the results of his travels. Stanley, was commissioned by New York Herald to undertake a secret mission to find and rescue the Scottish missionary David Livingstone, who was lost in the midst of the African jungle. Stanley describes his journey through the forests and rivers of Africa and his encounters with the African wildlife, tribespeople, and Arab settlers and traders amidst the variegated beauty of places such as Unyamwezi, Usagara, Ukawendi, and Tanganika districts. Ranging over such events such as Stanley's historic rescue of Livingstone to Livingstone's death and Stanley's further expeditions in Africa and his exploration and development of the Congo state, My African Travels is the saga of a passionate explorer with graphic descriptions of the vicissitudes of an African journey.

Cambridge University Press has long been a pioneer in the reissuing of out-of-print titles from its own backlist, producing digital reprints of books that are still sought after by scholars and students but could not be reprinted economically using traditional technology. The Cambridge Library Collection extends this activity to a wider range of books which are still of importance to researchers and professionals, either for the source material they contain, or as landmarks in the history of their academic discipline.

Drawing from the world-renowned collections in the Cambridge University Library, and guided by the advice of experts in each subject area, Cambridge University Press is using state-of-the-art scanning machines in its own Printing House to capture the content of each book selected for inclusion. The files are processed to give a consistently clear, crisp image, and the books finished to the high quality standard for which the Press is recognised around the world. The latest print-on-demand technology ensures that the books will remain available indefinitely, and that orders for single or multiple copies can quickly be supplied.

The Cambridge Library Collection will bring back to life books of enduring scholarly value (including out-of-copyright works originally issued by other publishers) across a wide range of disciplines in the humanities and social sciences and in science and technology.

My African Travels

HENRY MORTON STANLEY

CAMBRIDGE UNIVERSITY PRESS

Cambridge New York Melbourne Madrid Cape Town Singapore São Paolo Delhi

Published in the United States of America by Cambridge University Press, New York

www.cambridge.org
Information on this title: www.cambridge.org/9781108004114

© in this compilation Cambridge University Press 2009

This edition first published 1886
This digitally printed version 2009

ISBN 978-1-108-00411-4

MY

AFRICAN TRAVELS.

BY

H. M. STANLEY.

PRINTED FOR THE AUTHOR BY

WM. CLOWES & SONS, LIMITED, STAMFORD STREET

AND CHARING CROSS.

1886.

MY AFRICAN TRAVELS.

LADIES AND GENTLEMEN,

I propose to present you to-night with a short history of events that have transpired since 1870 in Equatorial Africa, and it may be, if you are devoid of prejudice in the matter, you will be able to perceive that the outcome of them may in time result in great good to the Dark Continent, and to its myriads of dark nations. By mere reiteration of the more uncomplimentary terms, people have sometimes half persuaded me that my enthusiasm has undermined my better judgment, and that I am an altogether unpractical man. However that may be, I will endeavour to place the more salient facts before you to-night in such a manner that each of the more attentive amongst you may be able to form a judgment upon the matter in much quicker time than I confess to have been able to form mine.

In 1869, while pursuing the avocations of a newspaper correspondent, dabbling in politics and other high matters with that self-sufficiency usual with young journalists, I was summoned by a brief telegram from my chief, Mr. Bennett, of the 'New York Herald,' to come to Paris without delay. On the second evening after the receipt of the telegraphic command, a personal

B

interview took place at the Grand Hotel. With characteristic abruptness, he informed me that the object for which he had sent for me was the search for an old traveller named David Livingstone, who, three years before, had disappeared in the wilds of Africa. Being naturally, by my profession, an omnivorous reader of all things with the least tincture of human interest in them, I immediately recollected that I had heard of the former existence of such a man, but beyond that he had been a missionary and traveller in Africa I possessed no knowledge of him. Mr. Bennett appeared to me to be much better informed, and in brief terms he condescended to enlighten me, and declared his conviction that the traveller was alive somewhere in the middle of the continent, and said he, in an electrifying manner, " I want you to proceed to Africa, and find him."

Let any young man here, however ambitious, try and put himself in my place. For instance, let him be a type-setter or daily reporter, clerk or cobbler, and let him fancy his employer declaring with the same startling abruptness his intention of sending him into the Polar Regions to discover the bones of Franklin, or into the middle of Africa to discover the relics of Hicks Pasha, and he will have an idea of the state of wonder I was in when I asked the great newspaper proprietor, " Right into the heart of Africa, Mr. Bennett?"

I have told the story frequently. I daresay you know it well. You know that I was rash enough to undertake the adventurous commission; that Mr. Bennett, with a prodigal generosity, placed thousands of pounds at my disposal; that he communicated some of his own enthusiasm into me, and that, in the white heat of it, I started the next day, with a budget of instructions which I look upon even to this day with dismay.

One after another I executed each of them: first, the Suez Canal reports; second, Upper Egypt and Baker's expedition; third, underground Jerusalem; fourth, politics in Syria; fifth, Turkish politics at Stamboul; sixth, archeological explorations in the Crimea; seventh, politics and progress in the Caucasus; eighth, projects of Russia; ninth, Trans-Caspian affairs; tenth, Persian politics and geography, and present condition; eleventh, Indian matters; twelfth, search for Dr. Livingstone throughout Equatorial Africa.

It was January 1871 before I arrived at Zanzibar to commence executing my last commission. Up to that date Livingstone had been fifty-eight months in the interior of Africa, and during nearly fifty months of which he had been lost to the ken of those who professed regard for him. Now cast your eyes over that huge configuration called Africa, or take the Equatorial portion of it. I knew he had entered it near S. lat. 10°; that he intended, after arriving at Nyassa Lake, to turn north-westerly. In fifty-eight months one might travel far, for even at a mile per day one could march 1750 miles. Measure about 1600 miles north-west, even from the south end of Nyassa Lake, and you will find a prong of your compasses resting on a point somewhere near 10° N. lat. But supposing that the traveller had marched at an average of two miles per day within the same period, he would have traversed as many degrees as he had been months away from the sea. Now fifty-eight degrees in a north-westerly direction from the southern end of Nyassa, would take one near the desert frontier of Algeria or Morocco, and the time I might occupy getting within a decent distance inland, he might utilize in reaching the Mediterranean Sea or some port on the North Atlantic Ocean.

Probably this method of describing the difficulty that now confronted me will suffice to bring the matter vividly home to your minds. I should also tell you that before arriving at Zanzibar it had not impressed itself sufficiently on my mind, that I should have to travel for many months, perhaps years, through lands inhabited by people whose complexion was of an alarming blackness, that the cream-coloured man would be more of a rarity with them than a coal-black man would be with us in England.

Nor had I thought to any great extent that all these black men were in a manner lawless; that many of them were savage; that some might be ferocious as wild dogs; that Africa possessed no theatres, newspapers, or agreeable society; and that a wheaten loaf could not be purchased with Rothschild's wealth. When I came face to face with the semi-naked blacks of Zanzibar, these horrors flashed upon me like a revelation. I felt I had been betrayed by rashness into a perilous as well as most disagreeable undertaking. Yet it was impossible to retire without making an effort. There was also some consolation in the thought that if my heart became too feeble in resolution, that I could return the way I went without any one being able to accuse me of returning from mere cowardice.

In due time the expedition was organized, and there was only one person at Zanzibar who understood the object of it. In a few weeks we began our march into the interior, and a few days later, despite the strangeness of the land and our surroundings, we had adjusted ourselves to our condition, and, after a manner, were content that fate had fixed us where it had. Very quickly the glamour that high and romantic expectations had cast over the country wore away. Game was not so plentiful as it might be; the forests and jungles were lovely to look at from the plain, but within they were full of creeping things and abominable insects, myriapedes and centipedes, ants and pismires, cobras and pythons. The branches distilled continually great drops of dew, which dripped on the road, the road become miry and slippery with the tread of many feet. Our bodies perspired intolerably in the warm air; our clothes galled us; our boots became limp and shapeless in the continual and everlasting mud. As we emerged from the jungle, and looked over the rolling plains, nothing could be more inviting than the prospect. We called it "park land" as we viewed it from a distance. But as we trod the too narrow path, meandering like a tortuous stream, and became hemmed in by tall coarse grass, with the fervid sun scorching our heads with its intolerable heat, attacked by gad-flies and hordes of persistent tsetse, our admiration of park land was not increased by our experience of its many discomforts; nor during the night, when with aching limbs, and half parboiled bodies, we sought well-earned repose, were we deprived of our quota of miseries, for red-water ants infested our bedding, mosquitos hung to our faces, crickets uttered their exasperatingly monotonous cricks, wood-ticks fastened on our bodies like

vampires, wild animals haunted the neighbourhood of our camp, hyænas laughed diabolically
outdoors, the nitrous earth exhaled its mephitic
vapours, until the night seemed to us to rival
the day in producing mortifying incidents.

Added to these were increasing troubles with
our carriers and animals. The stubborn pack-
donkeys continually contrived to upset the
loads of cloth in the mud; they sprawled over
the greasy, slippery roads as though they were
demented or drunk; the rain showered on us
daily, either soon after commencing a march,
or just before we could house ourselves and
goods; the porters threw away their packs
and deserted; the native chiefs took every occa-
sion to exact toll and irritate us by unceasing
demands on our store, and neither animate nor
inanimate nature appeared to us to favour our
wanderings.

We arrived at a great plain traversed by a
river called the Wami. The plain had been
inundated and was converted into a deadly
swamp. During the transit our poor asses died
daily; our porters and escort sickened and died;
and finally the Europeans lost heart and became
victims to the inclement season. There was a
time, when camped on the slopes of the Usagara
range, when the full sum of our troubles and
miseries was so great that but small inducement
was needed to cause us to abandon the heart-
breaking journey there and then. After a little
halt, however, on the mountain slopes, we felt
somewhat renovated. But as yet we had pene-
trated only 150 miles, which had occupied us
forty-three days in travelling.

We had not loitered on the way; on the con-
trary, the victims of the journey had been

numerous, man and beast had succumbed, but with the heartiest efforts to press on, the rate of travel did not exceed three and a half miles per day.

By this time the rainy season was over, the drenching rains had ceased, and a cool wind blew, the inundated plains and valleys of the maritime region were behind us. We were on the slopes of the mountain range, which when crossed would lead us into the more populous and drier regions of the African upland.

On the 8th May, 1871, we resumed our journey over the Usagara range, and in eight marches we arrived on the verge of the dry rolling plateau which continues almost without variety for nearly 600 miles westward. We soon after entered Ugogo, inhabited by a bumptious, full-chested, square-shouldered people, who exact heavy tribute on all caravans. Nine marches took us through their country, and when we finally shook the dust of its red soil off our feet, we were rich in the experience of native manners and arrogance, but considerably poorer in cloth.

Beyond Ugogo undulated the Land of the Moon or Unyamwezi, inhabited by a turbulent and combative race, who are as ready to work for those who can afford to pay as they are to fight those they consider unduly aggressive. Towards the middle of this land we came to a colony of Arab settlers and traders. Some of these have built excellent and spacious houses of sun-dried brick, and cultivate extensive gardens. The Arabs at that time were a hospitable people, and they made me welcome amongst them. We were now over 525 miles from the sea. The Arabs located here were great travellers. Every region round about had been diligently searched for ivory. Caravans departed and entered the colony at frequent intervals, two or three times week. If Livingstone was anywhere within reach some of these people ought surely to have known. But although I questioned eagerly all whom I came across, or became acquainted with, no one could give me definite information of the missing man.

While we were preparing to leave the Arab colony in Unyanyembe war broke out between the settlers and a native chief named Mirambo, and a series of sanguinary contests followed. In the hope that by adding my force to them a route west might be opened I foolishly enough joined them. We did not succeed, however, and a disastrous retreat followed. The country became more and more disturbed; bandits infested every road leading from the colony; cruel massacres, destruction of villages, raids by predatory Watuta were daily reported to us, until it seemed to us that there was neither means for advance nor retreat left. As our expedition had become thoroughly disorgan- ized, I might say annihilated, during our flight with the Arabs from the fatal cam- paign against Mirambo, I turned my atten- tion first to form another which, whether we should continue our search for the lost traveller, or abandon it, and turn our faces homeward, would be equally necessary, and as during such an unquiet period it would be a task requiring much time and patience, I meanwhile consulted my charts and the best-informed natives as to the possibility of evading the hostile bands of Mirambo by taking a circuitous route round the disturbed territory.

I just now mentioned that the distance from the sea to Unyanyembe was about 525 miles. We were delayed altogether at or near the Arab colony from the 23rd of June, 1871, to the 20th of September, eighty-nine days.

On this last date we resumed our journey with a new expedition, much smaller in numbers, but much stronger in discipline and means of defence. We had weeded out all the incapables, and all the ordinary unarmed porters, and instead of them we had men accustomed to travel, and to the vicissitudes of an African journey. I had also changed for the better. The raw youth who left the coast with a straggling caravan of 192 men of many tribes, willing to be guided by every hint the veteran porters had been pleased to give him, had, through bitter experience, been taught to lead his own force, and to exact ready and immediate obedience. Discipline over such a lawless mob as I had gathered from among the wilder spirits of Unyanyembe could not be enforced, of course, without a few tempestuous scenes, but by exhibiting liberality to the deserving, and severity to the more turbulent, long before we arrived at Lake Tanganika our expedition was a trained force, able to cope with the varied difficulties which beset a traveller in such wild regions without instantly dissolving at sight or hint of danger.

Lake Tanganika, and the Arab colony on its eastern shore around the port of Ujiji, were the objective point of this second journey. The distance between the two colonies by the circuitous route adopted was 450 miles, which occupied us 51 days, inclusive of marches and halts. Our rate of travel had thus improved to nine miles per day. To reach Ujiji from the sea we had travelled 975 miles in 235 days, of which 89 days had been consumed in delays at Unyanyembe, notwithstanding which, if we divide the total mileage by the number of days employed, our quotient will be about four and one-seventh miles a day.

But all this time we had heard nothing definite about the object of our search, until a few days off the port of Ujiji, when we met a native caravan which stated that a white man had appeared from the westward of the lake.

When standing on the last hill of all, enjoying the splendid view of the lake and the village of Ujiji half hidden in palm-groves a few hundred yards away, we announced our presence with volleys of musketry, and then resumed the line of march. Presently the inhabitants, informed by the customary volleys of the presence of a caravan, rushed out at first with alarm, because, as I have stated, Mirambo and his bandits had disturbed the entire country, and then with glad confidence to greet us. Among these were two black men, who to my astonishment greeted me in English and declared themselves to be servants of Dr. Livingstone. A few minutes later the long-lost traveller stepped out from his verandah, wondering at the news his servants brought him, much the same as I wondered at this remarkable and sudden termination of my search.

For only two months before I had written from Unyanyembe to the 'New York Herald,' "Good-bye, I am off the day after to-morrow for

Ujiji, Lake Tanganika; then perhaps to the Congo River, or elsewhere."

It was only the night previous, at Niamtaga, the last camp, that I had gossiped with my dark companions, and had told them that probably in two weeks' time we should be crossing Lake Tanganika for the continuation of the search of the lost traveller west of it.

But all at once, as though by a divine interposition, the object of our search was standing quietly in the market place of Ujiji. He had only arrived ten days previously from a long exploration of Manyema and the Trans-Tanganika regions, a wreck in body and fortune, to meet, all unknown to him, people possessing abundant means and necessaries of life, who were eagerly pressing from the East towards him, to offer them at his feet.

You can well imagine our mutual joy when a moment later we grasped one another's hands, and a pleasant intercourse, which lasted 124 days, was commenced then. About ten days later we were voyaging Lake Tanganika together, to explore the north end of that lake. We saw many a bit of exquisite scenery, of half-round bays backed by vivid green mountains. We were compelled to admire many a scene almost idyllic in its beauty. Still I was slow, despite Livingstone's efforts to interest me, to give my affections to Africa or things African. I received his lectures on the wondrous things he had witnessed in the little-known regions west of the lake with a manner resembling that with which you receive mine—quiet, attentive, but, I fear, somewhat incredulous and unsympathetic. Against his appeals to me in favour of Africa rose visions of the march from the sea; of a thousand unlovely incidents; of a myriad of dark faces, mainly hostile, at least brutish and ugly; memories of the pains and penalties paid by us on the journey, of losses of money and life; of dying forms of my companions, white and black; of broad expanses, waterless and productive of nothing but the acrid thorn-tree; of great stretches of country uncultivated and unattractive; and a deep impression within me of the utter joylessness of a life in those savage lands surrounded by a hundred lawless tribes, where human life was reckoned of less value than a fowl's. But during our wanderings around the lake, and back again to Unyanyembe, Livingstone returned at every opportunity to the charge of converting me from my bitter dislike of the people and the land, or rather of endeavouring to teach me to view them with less prejudiced eyes. Fever, suffering, grief, trouble, hunger, and thirst, which like others I was compelled to endure, were urging me on the other side not to yield to his persuasive arguments. I finally left him comfortable and full of hope of better things for Africa at Unyanyembe, while I hastened seaward to fit out another expedition for him. I must confess to you that though I wished well to the continent for which he was labouring, I was strong in the conviction that he was engaged in a hopeless task, for a thankless people.

It is true that I had viewed lands which appeared to be valuable. Usagara was lovely— only a degree less lovely than Switzerland. Unyamwezi contained many scenes eminently pastoral. Ukawendi rejoiced in forested hills, valleys, and plains, of which something might be made, provided that they were easily accessible. The Tanganika districts, so far as nature was concerned, were equal to anything on the shores of Lake Geneva, but they were environed by so many other disadvantages that obscured their special beauties.

On the 21st September, 1874, thirty-one months from the date of my parting with Livingstone, I was again in Zanzibar. Meantime Livingstone had died near Lake Bangweolo, and his body had been brought to England and buried in Westminster Abbey, and I had written the records of my search for him, and had subsequently gone through a few more experiences in Africa with Wolseley's expedition to Coomassie.

I was now about to prepare an expedition that had for its object the exploration of Lake Victoria, the circumnavigation of Lake Tanganika, and the descent of that great river discovered by Livingstone flowing north some 300 miles west of Lake Tanganika. If successful, I should set at rest several important geographical problems. There were some savants who persisted in declaring Lake Victoria to consist of a cluster of small lakes, separated by broad swamps; the outlet to Lake Tanganika was still undiscovered; and it was a disputable question which of the great rivers, Nile, Niger, or Congo, received the wide Lualaba, discovered by Livingstone.

A battalion of 356 men was organized to convey beads, wire, cloth, scientific instruments, photographic apparatus, books, tools, and a miscellaneous variety of property necessary for a long journey and important work. We also transported a cedar boat 40 feet long by 6 feet

D

beam, cut up in sections for portage, for the exploration of the great lakes.

As far as the westernmost frontier of Ugogo the route followed by the second expedition was nearly similar to the one travelled by the first. We then plunged into a wilderness, and as our faithless guides had deserted us, we endured great distress and many privations. Nine of our party perished from hunger and fatigue; a few were irretrievably lost. Out of this terrible waste we emerged after nine days' march, to find ourselves in a populous country, remarkable for the nakedness and determined ferocity of its people, and also for being the locality whose marshes and wooded hills and plains, 5300 feet above sea-level, gave birth to the extremest springs of the Nile. For ten days we lived amongst these people, expecting to hear every moment the peculiar *oi-yoi* which with them signalled war. Every art was exhausted to prolong the truce which we felt existed between us from the moment that we entered their territory, and if the peace had depended upon the conduct of the Europeans, it might have continued unbroken unto this day, but when we consider that a trivial squabble with the smallest boy in the expedition was quite sufficient to precipitate the conflict with such aggressive people, you may better understand what reason I had for anxiety.

On the eleventh morning the outbreak took place, and one of our men was speared to death whilst collecting fuel; a sick man lagging behind the caravan was vindictively hacked to pieces. Over two thousand naked warriors surrounded our astonished camp, and in a short time both parties were engaged. My losses amounted to 21 dead before sunset. What the

natives lost we never knew. The second day
the conflict was resumed, with less loss on our
side, and on the third day the natives advanced,
only to be utterly discouraged by their losses
before night. About midnight we departed out
of our camp, and thirty-six hours later we
arrived in the friendly country of Usukuma,
which stretched to the Victorian fresh-water
sea, nearly 260 miles. You may thus imagine
the ample extent of the country we had now
entered. It was while traversing through Usukuma that I first awoke to the bare possibility
that some portions of Equatorial Africa might
really be worth serious attention from Europe.
As day after day we pressed on towards the great
lake, the beautiful and green rolling land was
seen to expand on either side, dotted with
villages, and browsing herds of cattle. The
healthful and cool breezes bore to us the grateful
smell of fresh young grass, and the delicious
home-farm odour of cattle suggestive of abundance of milk and luscious cream. Amiable
natives offered their strong backs to assist our
tired people, and from one end of Usukuma to
the lake shores, we knew but little trouble or
anxiety. Indeed, when at last after 103 days of
march, at a distance of 720 miles from the ocean,
we viewed the grey waters of the Great Lake, we
fully sympathized with the Usukuma minstrel
as he sang to us on the 27th of February, 1875,

" Lift up your heads, O men, and gaze around;
　Try if you can see its end.
　See, it stretches moons away,
　This great and sweet fresh-water sea.

　We come from Usukuma Land,
　Land of pastures, cattle, sheep, and goats,
　Land of braves, warriors and strong men,
　And lo! this is the far-known Usukuma Sea."

Of the dangers and the severity of the task of circumnavigation of Lake Victoria undertaken by us soon after arriving on its shores, it is not my purpose to speak, as time would not permit me, but in order that my narrative though brief may be consistent, I may tell you, that after a voyage of nearly 1100 miles around the lake, we ascertained this body of fresh water to be 21,500 square miles in extent, which approaches approximately to twice the superficial area of Wales.

For a second time, after considering the various countries round about it, their natural resources and peoples, the conviction gradually came to my mind that Livingstone after all was not very wrong when he tried to persuade me that there were vast expanses in Africa fit for the white man to live in, without which of course civilization for Africa was for ever impossible. And yet Livingstone had never been within 600 miles of the southern end of this lake, when expatiating upon the merits of the continent. Uganda appeared to me, compared with the barbarity and ferocity I had witnessed elsewhere, to be a semi-civilized country. I estimated its population at about 3,000,000, and over all reigned a despotic monarch more inclined than any of his people to the arts of civilization. He made such an impression upon me that I advised English people to send a mission out to him. The Church Missionary Society responded to the call, and some of its members who arrived in Uganda in 1877 still live there. Mtesa, the Emperor of Uganda, to whom the mission was sent, died last year, his successor, I regret to say, being but a youth, and influenced by the more conservative pagans of the court, distinguished himself soon after by the murder of Bishop Hannington and his party, though the Bishop cannot be said to have been quite prudent in the route he chose to enter Uganda. Africans, however, would be less than men if they did not struggle, as the ancient Romans did, against the advances of Christianity.

I also discovered that from its extreme southern sources the Nile had a winding course of 4200 miles, and that it flowed direct across 2221 miles of latitude, and that, though not the largest, it is certainly the second longest river in the world.

From the north-western extremity of the Victoria Nyanza, we made a journey westward in the latter part of 1875, and discovered a new lake, called by the natives Muta Nzigé. We were unable to proceed further in that direction, and retraced our steps to the Victoria, and the beginning of the year 1876 was occupied by us in exploring the region lying between the Victoria Lake and the extensive kingdom of Ruanda. Thence we travelled to Lake Tanganika, which we also undertook to circumnavigate. This last body of water we discovered to be about 7300 square miles in extent; being 363 miles long, by an average breadth of 20.

While the grey Nyanza, named Victoria, expands to a breadth almost equal to its length, the Tanganika Lake occupies a huge crevasse, deeply sunk between lofty mountains, rising from 1000 feet to 3000 above its dark blue waves.

We arrived at Ujiji, the place where I had met Livingstone forty-three months before, on the 27th of May, 1876, and two months later we left it for the last time, to set about resolving the mystery of the Lualaba, Livingstone's great river.

After crossing Tanganika, and getting behind or west of its western mountainous shore, I was at once struck with the great difference that existed between the colouring of the vegetation and the general aspect of the country we now looked upon, to that which we had but lately left. East, the land was blackened with the ashes of the burnt grass, the leaves of trees hung brown, and scorched, and dead, amid desolation; but west of Tanganika the whole region was in a state of verdant luxuriance—all nature rejoiced in a full spring-time. Palms were abundant; out of every copse and jungle the rattan waved its delicate and fringed head; gigantic ferns, amoma, and wild banana intensified the vivid verdure of the underwood; orchids bloomed in the tree forks; green mosses shrouded the sober colouring of the forest monarchs; creepers dangled in festoons, and wove graceful leafy chaplets between them, as though animate nature welcomed spring in the same manner as man welcomes the conqueror. East of the Tanganika the palm family was rare, and between the maritime region and the lake I do not remember to have seen one.

As we continued our journey westward the land became more gracious and generous. An interesting diversity of hill and dale, valley and plain, marked it. Some rare and lovely scenes were viewed. While vegetation astonished us by its prodigious growth, height, and density, by the new forms of life which it assumed, man in his habits was also changed; his ideas of architecture were different; to strangers he appeared strange himself among his own kind, but exhibited more promising qualities as a progressive being.

His ironwork, carving in wood, his tools and utensils, his warlike weapons, his domestic arrangements and contrivances, even his mode of personal adornment, were all superior to his dark brother who dwelt on the eastern side of the Tanganika.

His diet had also changed. To the east of the lake he maintained himself on grain chiefly; to the west he lived on cassava and bananas. The goats of the west were also of a peculiar breed, and double the size of the eastern goat, and the sheep were of the broad-tailed and maned species.

He made his cloth of different materials. Instead of the felt-like cloth obtained from the inner bark of a tree, he wove pleasant and pliant drapery from strange grasses, and decorated them in colours, and with fringes. Indeed in many ways the contrast was as strong as that which exists between southern Europe and northern Africa.

Even the animals of the wilds had changed. Instead of the black buffalo we met the fawn or reddish kind; instead of the dog-faced baboon, the soko or chimpanzee prevailed; instead of the smooth-haired kudu, the long-haired water-buck predominated; the lion had been replaced by the spotted leopard, and lynx; jackals and hyænas were not known; zebra, and giraffe, and gnu, with the bulkier rhinoceros, were hardly ever seen, while the elephant reigned sole king of the animal kingdom.

This abrupt change in man, in the vegetable and animal kingdom—to be more definite—commenced at the watershed dividing streams flowing westward from those flowing into the lake. From the watershed the land inclined with a gentle descent towards the broad trough of the Lualaba, and our path westward almost followed the windings of its tributary, the Luama, from its source to the confluence.

The great river which had been such a mystery to Livingstone at this point, showed a superb breadth of 1400 yards. A few days later we arrived at Nyangwe, the furthest point Livingstone attained, and whence he returned in 1871, on that dismal tramp to Ujiji, to find me ten days later in search of him.

You will remember we started from the Indian Ocean with a force of 356 men: this had dwindled by this time to 146 men, women, and children. From Nyangwe, straight easterly across the continent to the ocean, the distance is 880 miles, but straight westerly to the Atlantic Ocean the distance is 1070 miles.

Thus we had not yet reached the centre of the continent by 100 miles, though we had occupied 706 days in arriving thus far. Nine days after our arrival at Nyangwe we commenced the journey across the western half of Africa. By good fortune we succeeded in securing the escort of a wealthy Arab merchant and his band of 700 people for a short distance to inspire my own men with a little courage, since, of course, as they had listened eagerly to the wondrous stories told by natives and Arabs relating to the countries we were about to explore, their imaginations had exaggerated the terrors we should experience.

From the bright and sunny district of Nyangwe we entered the forest land of Manyema and Uregga, a gloomy region involved in twilight, and fable. Down every tree and branch and leaf trickled the dewdrops like a light summer rain ; the damp earth exhaled the dew back again in a warm vapour, which filled the lower atmosphere, became distilled into water again, before it could emerge above the dense mass of forest leafage, to fall once more in a continued shower of warm drops. Trampled by the feet of a column of nearly 850 people, the path soon became mud, through which we splashed and sprawled, wet to the skins, and bathed in profuse perspiration. This experience lasted fifteen days, and we sought the great river once more to seek relief from our sufferings, and from the terrible strain on the physical system.

It was then I launched my boat on the river—the boat that we had brought with us from England, the same that had circumnavigated the Lakes Victoria, Windemere and Tanganika; the same that had voyaged on the Alexandra Nile, and had enabled us to cross many a rapid stream. By purchase we acquired five canoes from the natives before long, and forming a river and a land force, we commenced the descent of the river.

As this was an unusual scene to the natives, they used all their arts to impede us. By land and water, night and day, they sought by every means to drive us back. Sickness aided them greatly, and day after day the great river received the victims of the journey. At the distance of 215 miles from Nyangwe, our Arab escort declined to go further, because the losses in life were so appalling. Human endurance, they said, could go no further, nor was Arab valour of any avail against half a continent peopled with such savages. We accordingly released them from their contract, and parted,

F

not without a foreboding that we would never
see one another in this world again.

My people, however they might feel at the
word of command, cried out Bismillah!—in the
name of God—and the desperate voyage down the
unknown river began. Here we were like one
family 140 strong, with hearts united in the strong
purpose to reach the sea, and home. The swift
flood bore us northward resistlessly, while our
friends turned their faces eastward. Presently
we approached villages, the war cries were
uttered, and in fierce concert the natives, gaily
feathered for the fight, dashed out towards us.
They were scattered in short time, and we continued our way, leaving them wondering and
lamenting. A few miles below, the villages
from either bank again despatched their quota
of eager warriors, only, however, to fall back
bruised and disheartened, but not too discouraged to send after us pealing notes of
defiance and hatred. The river expanded in
breadth with every new affluent; each shore
presented a bank of massive forest of primeval
luxuriance and thickness; but every few miles
a cluster of villages were seen, sometimes on one
side, sometimes on the other, sometimes on
both, and each cluster despatched a force to
dispute the passage. Drums beat, horns blew,
prolonged savage cries, which were echoed by
the thick forests, a splashing of hundreds of
paddles, and then volleys of musketry drowned
all with their crackling explosions. Such were
the sounds that now disturbed the silence of the
broad river, that had brooded in mysterious
seclusion during the preceding ages.

In the midst of our exciting troubles with
the human aborigines of these new lands, some

hills were seen ahead, breaking the monotony of the level and wooded banks, and in a short time we heard a deep murmur of waters, which as we approached filled the air with its sullen boom. Jets of spray were seen shooting up across the river; wreaths of white vapour curled above the fall; the roar become louder, an increasing velocity of the current was observable. With hearts verging on despair, but resolute to struggle, we faced the shore where the native warriors were assembled to witness our plunge over the fall, and yell a requiem over the hated strangers.

Then began a struggle with the furious flood, and ferocious savages, which lasted twenty-two days, and extended over fifty miles, without scarcely any intermission; but on the 28th January, 1877, we had passed the last of the Stanley Falls, reduced in numbers, it is true, but still formidable to resist the attacks of such people as we encountered. We were now 385 miles north of Nyangwe. It will be remembered that on account of its persistent flow to the northward, Livingstone believed that the great river belonged to the Nile; that neither natives nor Arabs at Nyangwe could say more than that the river flowed north. In its course beyond Nyangwe, in a distance of 385 miles, we ascertained that its course had only inclined forty miles westward.

Now, however, after leaving the Stanley Falls, we perceived a deflection to the west-north-west, between hilly banks, clad in impenetrable woods.

We were once more afloat in our boat and canoes on a mighty and navigable stream, whose grey-brown waters bore us downward still deeper

into the bosom of the unknown. We were not
a whit dejected after our late terrible experiences
and losses. Disquiet and melancholy were
banished by the novelties of the hitherto undiscovered lands. The strifeful days gave
us no opportunity to brood, and bewail our
rashness in adventuring the descent of the
unknown river. Our purpose was still as
strong as ever for gliding down, and to strive,
and seek, and find, and not to yield, even though
we died.

From the 28th of February to the 13th of
March, a period of 44 days, we paddled down, as
I said, a west-north-west course, then west,
then south-westerly, a distance of nearly 1100
miles, our descent uninterrupted by the river,
but harassed frequently by the native tribes.
First the Bakusu with great gallantry dashed on
our flanks, and skirmished with us incessantly;
then from the Aruwimi descended the Basoko,
a mighty host of plumed warriors in magnificent war-canoes, then the Bauru, and
the Wakatakura, the Barangi, the Wabika.
After these the Bangala, a populous tribe
armed with muskets, dashed out on us
in sixty-three canoes, and maintained a fierce
fight, lasting six hours. After passing these, the
Wakomera and the Byyanzi took pot shots at
us, as we glided by their settlements. Below
them the Bateké tried once by surprise to over-
power us, but arriving in that great expansion
of the river known as Stanley Pool, a little
acquaintance with the natives informed us that
the gauntlet was run, for we now heard delighted
natives talk freely of white men, of cloth, and
barter, and the ocean.

I have said that we were 44 days paddling

down this magnificent stretch of navigable water. One-half the time you may say we were engaged in furious contests with the natives, who from every settlement darted out to the attack of the strangers, but during the other half we had abundance of leisure to meditate as we floated down past the eerie isles, and unbroken forests which clothed them. From the half-mile breadth which it maintained a few miles below the Stanley Falls, affluent after affluent, mostly first-class tributaries, had swelled the volume of the river until in some places it had expanded into the enormous breadth of 16 miles, divided by a series of lengthy islands into from five to eight different channels. When it inclined west-north-west, a suspicion that, after all, it might be the Niger that we were exploring, for a time crept into my mind; but when it rolled westward, doubt took possession of me; when it turned south-west the mystery was resolved, and we then knew that the Lualaba of Livingstone was the upper portion of the Congo.

In our intervals of leisure, as we glided down mid the Sabbath serenity of the unpeopled islands, and the dreamy stillness of the primeval wilds, pondering upon the revelations which were daily growing into a higher importance on my new map, we speculated on the uses which such a river might be put to, provided that we were not interrupted by cataracts in our descent. As the miles began to number hundreds, anxiety on this score became intense; our prayer, while everything was yet blank as futurity before us, was, "Let the mileage grow on, let it increase, good Lord, and extend to thousands, without which the continent is lost for ever!" Steadily it lengthened ; day after day, in due order and rank, the mighty tributaries entered the parent river, and amplified its breadth. From the far north and the distant south, through the regions of many a dark potentate of Lunda and Rua, through the lands bordering on Moslem territory, dark waters from the south, milk-white waters from the north, the tributaries came, and silently emptied their treasures of water into its depth. I felt as though a witness of the creation of a new world, anxious that it should be a masterpiece to be hailed as the home of new nations. Glorious in vegetation, unequalled in its tropical verdure, remarkable for its variety of herb and leaf, generous in its promise of unbounded fruitfulness, beautiful in its budding bloom, the land went softly gliding by our eyes, mile after mile, until a thousand miles had been counted. Soon after we emerged from between mountainous banks, and entered the stately expanse of the Pool. At its western extremity, after a gentle flow of 1070 miles, the Congo narrowed again, and presently the hoarse sound of falling waters was heard, and vaporous clouds were seen as the river sullenly plunged down the long series of rapids, known as the Livingstone Falls, and we knew that the utmost limit of navigation was reached.

We still clung to the river, hoping against hope that another valuable stretch of navigation would be discovered. Month after month we toiled on, until in the fifth month we abandoned our canoes and our faithful boat and began our overland march, which ended after 60 miles at Boma on the Lower Congo, on the 9th August, 1877. Two days later we arrived at the Atlantic Ocean, a small force numbering 114, having occupied 999 days in the journey of 7158 miles long through the Dark Continent.

After a sufficient rest, I began the preparation of my map, in order to see what was the gain of our long journey. You will remember that when with Livingstone I was a strong sceptic as to the value of Africa, and though I deferred to his greater knowledge of it, with the courage of ignorance, I was prompt in giving proofs that to men equally ignorant with myself would have appeared unanswerable. When the map was finished, and I regarded the 30,000 square miles of lakes, and that splendid river, with its length of 3200 miles, which we had just descended, and speculated as to the thousands of miles of navigation which its noble tributaries would furnish over and above its own, and remembered the countless tropical treasures I had viewed, and the vast area of fertile land, great enough for a mighty empire, and thought of the millions of dark men I had seen, and considered what might be created by their muscles if rightly directed, then was I rebuked by my own work for my scepticism, for behold, I saw only the development and corroboration of Livingstone's ideas and words! Like the child to whom the alphabet at first was a mystery, no sooner has he learned the art of reading than he wonders how he had scorned it, so I after some five years of training in the university of African travel wondered at my former doubts and little faith in the value of Africa.

Hitherto as you see, I had been only a student in this field of research, but on my arrival in England I became a teacher. I was eager to teach people here that in Western

Africa the largest river of the continent emptied itself into the sea through a land that knew no owner. True, it had a claimant in Portugal, but nobody outside of Portugal recognized such a claim. I said, " You will proceed to annex it if you are wise, lest you be forestalled, for other nations are stirring and striving. It is a grand market for your cloth manufactures. Those dark millions require clothing and ornament, guns and powder, knives and needles, pottery and glassware, and they have rich products of ivory, and rubber, and dyes, and gums, and oils to exchange for them, and in barter there is great profit." As you may imagine, having been myself so slow to believe, I was not greatly surprised that those concerned in England with such things were equally slow to learn. But across the Channel in Belgium, King Leopold was a great reader of explorations, and an earnest student of geography. He soon arrived at a conception of this case of discovery, and summoning me to Brussels, he placed in my hands a commission to return to the Congo to explore more closely the commercial resources of the country, and to ascertain what protection could be given to commercial enterprise by native chiefs, and how intercourse and traffic could best be encouraged and promoted.

On the 19th of January, 1879, I set out from England on my last journey. I first proceeded to Zanzibar, and enlisted nearly seventy men, about forty of whom had followed me across Africa. Returning by way of the Mediterranean with these men, we steamed southerly from Gibraltar, along the west coast of Africa, and arrived at the mouth of the Congo about the middle of August. By this time I had gathered an expedition consisting of 14 Europeans and 210 negroes. For the first few weeks we were employed in launching and preparing our four little steamers for their work. We then steamed up the Congo, and in order to put as great a distance as possible between ourselves and the mercantile factories on the lower river we occupied ground at a place called Vivi, at the head of navigation on the Lower Congo. After a cession of the district of Vivi, duly made by the natives to us, we proceeded to erect our first station of wooden huts that were purchased in England and had been shipped to us, and to make waggon-roads in the neighbourhood, for easy transit of the steamers for the start of the overland journey. At the end of January 1880 Vivi station was completely established. A short journey was now necessary to decide upon the best route to the interior, and on our return from it we commenced the labour of making a waggon-road to Isangila, our second station. By the last day of the year the second station was also completed. Computing by statute miles the various marchings and as frequent countermarchings accomplished during the year, I find they amount to a total of 2352 English miles according to tape-line measurement of foot by foot, making an average of six and a half miles throughout every day in the year. All this only to gain an advance into the interior of 52 miles! During this work six Europeans and twenty-two natives perished through climate and fatigue.

At Isangila we made a similar treaty with the natives as at Vivi, and obtained a concession of land.

We then set about establishing a third station, distant 88 miles by river from Isangila.

H

Two steamers and two lighters were launched on the river, to be occupied in conveying about 50 tons of stores and tools. Within 70 days we arrived safely with all our waggons and goods, at Manyanga, having travelled up and down the river in 14 voyages a distance of 2464 miles. We were yet only 140 miles from Vivi, and this had occupied us 436 days in road-making, and conveying steamers and 50 tons of miscellaneous property.

At Manyanga fever delayed us a great deal. We were short of men. Vivi, Isangila, and Manyanga required to be garrisoned, and these had taken a great number of valuable men from our working force.

By the 1st of July, however, the third station was approaching completion. Eight days later I was at Stanley Pool surveying the country for a road, and to negotiate for ground to build the Supply Station for the Upper Congo. But the north bank had already been ceded to France through the enterprise of Mons. de Brazza, who had in some manner been informed of my purpose. Perceiving that I was too late to secure the north bank, I negotiated with the natives on the south bank, and was assured that the only cession that should be made, would be to us. We retraced our steps to Manyanga, and commenced removing our material and hauling our steamers overland towards Stanley Pool.

A reinforcement from Zanzibar just then arrived, which gave us great encouragement, and so great was the influence of this accession to our strength that by the 3rd of December, 1881, we had launched one steamer and boat on the Upper Congo, and all our weighty impedimenta were safely stored in our tented village, which was afterwards replaced by the station of Leopoldville. By the 1st of February, 1882, the officers' house and magazine were completed.

We now turned our attention to arrange caravans for maintaining communication at regular periods between the sea and Stanley Pool, to extend our influence around, and to obtain as much territory as possible from the native chiefs, and in instructing officers in their new duties. Our line of communication was as follows. From the port of Banana at the mouth of the Congo to Vivi, our steamer, the *Belgique*, made regular trips every alternate day. Land caravans of porters conveyed goods overland to Isangila. Thence a large lighter was rowed up stream to Manyanga, and from thence caravans conveyed the goods overland to Leopoldville at Stanley Pool. The length of the line from the sea to Leopoldville was 343 miles, or a twenty days' journey.

On the 19th of April we set about establishing a fifth station near the junction of the Kwa with the Congo. A steamer, towing a whaleboat and two canoes, conveyed the force and the material required. We occupied seven days in reaching the locality. Eleven days were employed in the negotiations that followed, as a great deal of patient palavering was needed for both parties to arrive at a thorough under-standing.

We returned to Leopoldville to obtain men, goods, and Europeans for the establishment of a sixth station, but on arriving there no Europeans were available. However as they were reported to be on the road, we loaded the boats with goods and men, and conveyed them to the fifth station. Then, in order to occupy the time in useful work, I steamed up the Kwa tributary to explore that river. At the distance of 220 miles from the mouth, I discovered the river to widen gradually until we emerged upon a lake. As I had heard no rumour of it whatsoever, I regarded it as a piece of geographical good luck. Following closely the right shore, I could faintly distinguish the outlines of the left shore, but at certain places nothing of it could be seen, proving that it must be irregular in outline. Briefly I may say that after its circumnavigation, we found it to be 70 miles in length, with a breadth varying between 6 and 38 miles, surrounded by a splendid forest country, alternating with undulating grass lands.

On my return from the examination of the lake, I was struck down with a violent fever, which rendered me a helpless invalid for some weeks. After appointing another gentleman to take command in my absence, I returned to Europe. Within six weeks I was so far recovered as to be enabled to return again to the Congo, and on the 20th December I was back at Vivi once more, after an absence of about four months.

With the beginning of 1883 we began a more active acquisition of territory for the Association Internationale Africaine. I despatched an expedition to the Lower Kwilu, another to the Niadi-Kwilu, another along the south bank of the Congo, and a fourth to Stanley Pool, to purchase all those portions of lands lying between the districts conceded already to us, in order to make them all one continuous territory.

Before the end of the first month of my

return to the Congo I led a fifth expedition,
conveying another steamer to the Upper Congo.
On the 9th of May, 1883, I started up-river with
three steamers, towing a whaleboat and large
canoe, manned by 80 men, and provisioned for
six months. The latter part of that month we
were occupied in settling affairs at the station
of Bolobo, and reducing the fractious natives
around to more pacific relations with the
garrison. Through the month of June we were
employed in negotiating with Lukolela, Irebu,
and the Bakuti, in building the station of
Equator-ville, and in exploring the Buruki
River and Mantumba Lake.

From July to the middle of August we were
engaged in repairing our steamers, refitting, and
reloading for another long voyage. The following five months were employed by us in negotiations with the tribes between Equatorville,
and Stanley Falls. On the left bank, Lukolela
accepted a station ; Inganda, Uranga, Bolombo,
begged hard that we should settle among them
on the north bank, the Bangala and Wapoto
ceded territories. At Yambinga we entered into
friendly relations, the Basoko submitted peace-
fully and expressed their willingness to become
more intimate with us. Between the Basoko
and Stanley Falls we found the villages reduced
to ashes by a series of slave raids by the Arabs,
but at Stanley Falls, with the willing consent of
the natives, we established a station and left a
garrison to guard it. It was then I considered
my work ended. The rest was a were matter of
detail. Over 400 chiefs had consented to treat
with us, and to cede the government of their
lands into our hands. The treaties were
drawn up in the most stringent manner, by

I

which the destiny of the Congo banks had been given to the Association. No political agent in future could enter in the guise of a guest, with a blank treaty and a national flag, without being guilty of treason. We had been engaged in building a State, and it behoved us to fence it round with all measures calculated to secure it from disturbance during its period of infancy. With the exception of a small portion of the Lower Congo, and a fraction of the north bank of Stanley Pool, the territory of the Congo basin belonged to the Association and its power also extended to the entire basin of the Kwilu-Niadi.

In June 1884, after surrendering the command of the Congo territory to Colonel de Winton, I returned to Europe. Until February 1885, we were engaged in negotiations with the European Powers to secure the recognition of the right of the International Association to govern the Congo territories. On the 26th of February, 1885, the Plenipotentiaries subscribed their names and seals to the General Act of the Berlin Conference, establishing with mutual goodwill most favourable conditions for commerce and free navigation on the Congo and the Niger, and in the meantime, by separate conventions with the several Powers, the Association was recognised as an African Power, and its territories on the Congo as a free and independent State. A few months later the Royal founder of this great work was permitted by his own people to add to his title of King of the Belgians that of the Sovereign of the Independent State of the Congo.

During last year a Government was constituted, which consists of King Leopold and a

Council of Administrators-General, who are the heads of various State Departments. That of Foreign Affairs includes also the Department of Justice, of the Post-office and commercial matters. That of Finance also includes that which relates to tribal and alien landed interests and State domains. That of the Interior includes all matters relating to its administration, roads, industries, police and transport services—the personnel and materiel for the defence of the State. The Government of the State is located in Brussels, in two buildings, near King Leopold's palace. On the Congo, the Executive Power, charged with the execution of such laws and orders as may be decreed by the Government at Brussels, consists of an Administrator-General, assisted by a Vice-Administrator, a Director of Finance, and Chief Justice. The European force in charge of the stations, steamers, and boats, number between 90 and 100. The armed police varies between 300 and 500. These are judiciously scattered along the land-route at various points. The transport service is regularly conducted on the lower river by three steamers—one of 100 tons, another of 20 tons, and a third of 8 tons. The goods and materiel are then transported overland by organised caravans of native porters — each caravan, which departs weekly, and sometimes oftener, conveying from two to eight tons, according to its numerical force. At Stanley Pool, after fifteen days' carriage overland, the merchandise and stores are warehoused, until they are taken up-river by the Upper Congo flotilla, which consists of four steamers, and distributed among the different posts established on the two banks of the river.

Up to the present time the State has been supported exclusively from King Leopold's private means, the annual maintenance fund devoted by him being fixed at £40,000. As however, the State has commenced to levy export duties, its revenue will probably be increased to £50,000 this year.

For the purpose of examining what the prospects of its future prosperity are likely to be, let us divide the State into three divisions: the Lower Congo, the Cataract region, and the Upper Congo.

The Lower Congo is navigable for 110 miles, but only its north bank, with a limited depth inland, and a strip of five miles on the south bank, near the rapids, belong to the Congo State. More than one-half of it is an unsightly, and rugged hill land, unproductive to labour, and extremely unhealthy, owing to the chill winds blowing from the South Atlantic, which produce a remarkable variation of temperature. In any place sheltered from the sea wind, the sun's heat soon excites perspiration, and an uncomfortable warmth; but on stepping into the open, the cold winds, though grateful for the moment, soon cause that shivering preliminary of fever. The other half consists mainly of waste plain and marsh lands, and fertile valleys where the natives plant ground-nuts, and build their villages, in the shade of palm-groves. From the palms they obtain a wine-juice called malafu. These palm-nuts furnish yellow fat, for the manufacture of lubricants and soap, and the kernels are exported to make feed-cake for cattle. Along some portions of the north and south bank a few factories have been established which support themselves by exchanging cloth, cutlery, crockery, and gin, for the simple products, ground-nuts, palm-oil and kernels. Thus you may perceive that the region of the Lower Congo presents nothing very promising in the future.

Turning to the Cataract region, which you must traverse afoot, there being no beast capable of being used for transport, we observe still less to ensure a hopeful future for the State. True, in area it is somewhat greater, being 140 miles long by 110 miles wide, covering 15,400 square miles. But its population is scanty and the country is irregular, broken up into a succession of steep hills and valleys, in the main producing dense crops of tall grass, especially in bottom lands. Over this area are scattered every few miles the native villages, either in clusters or isolated, each with its palm-grove, its ground-nut plots, and its cassava gardens. The country is well watered and each stream has its banks lined with timber. Here and there quite a forest may be seen, and the hollows which have received the humus from the uplands, nourish thick woods which are rendered almost impenetrable by a rank undergrowth of creepers and bush. The products of the country are ground-nuts, palm-oil and kernels, rubber, gum-copal, and ivory. The three first will not pay transport by carriers; as there is no systematic search for copal and rubber, these may not be depended upon, and the ivory—though there are still many herds of elephants roaming through it—is not so plentiful as to make trade in it encouraging.

The road through this region, which continually runs up and down steep slopes for a distance of 235 miles, is a mere footpath, choked by rank growths of giant grasses, and hemmed

K

in by bush, painful for the foot traveller, whether
it is over the naked quartz-cobble hill, or
through the suffocating grassy tunnels of the
plains and bottom lands. Few men after
marching through this region can have much
love for it, since it has cost them serious physical
pain and toil. By the time they have reached
the borders of the third region, their energies
and constitutions have been so weakened, and
their misery has been so great, that few of them
are capable of examining, without prejudice, the
most interesting and the thousandfold more
valuable region of the Upper Congo.

I venture to say, that if Stanley Pool were
the sea-port of West Equatorial Africa, and the
navigation of the Upper Congo were accessible
to the trader's steamer, the Congo basin would
long have been on the high road to civilization.
But between that circular expansion of the great
African river, whence begins that vast mileage
that I shall presently refer to, and the sea, there
is a terraced steep, nearly a hundred and fifty
miles long, and nearly threescore of rapids,
which render navigation impossible.

At the western extremity of Stanley Pool
begins, therefore, this third region, accessible, as
I told you, after steaming 110 miles, and after a
land march of 235, or say 345 miles from the sea.
From the landing place at the Pool we may now
take passage on a tolerably commodious steamer
and travel uninterruptedly up the main stream
for 1070 miles, then up the Lubiranzi tributary
for 250 miles, up the Lulungu 300 miles, the
Black River 300 miles; we may voyage up the
Kwa River, steam round the shores of Lake
Leopold 350 miles, and then up the Kwa-Kassai
400 miles, and up its tributaries 300 miles.

Lake Mantumba's wooded shores present a water-front of 70 miles; and if we choose to visit the northern portion of the basin the Lawson-Lufini, the Mikene-Alima, the Bunga-Likona, the Ubangi, Ngala, Itimbiri, Biyerre, and Chofu tributaries will give us access for 1200 miles. The main stream and greater tributaries mentioned furnish us in the aggregate with over 4000 miles. These only have thus far been explored, but the explorers to whom we are indebted for the information lead us to believe that half as much again will be discovered before long. As my successor, Sir Francis de Winton, said in his address to the Geographical Society, lately—"It is the missionary Grenfell's opinion, and I coincide with him, that when this region is fully explored it will be found that there is scarcely a hundred miles of its area which is not approachable by a water-way."

The area referred to lies between E. longitude 15° 30′ and 26° 30′, and S. latitude 6° and N. latitude 5°, making a perfect square 759 miles either way, giving us a superficial extent of 576,000 square miles. As we are certain of finding at least 6000 miles of uninterrupted navigation, the statement of Messrs. Grenfell and De Winton is confirmed. Taking village by village from Stanley Pool to Stanley Falls, along 1070 miles of the main river, I estimated the population of both banks to be 632,000, which would give us 245 souls to every mile of river-bank. Along the Biyerre River banks I found the population dense enough to give 492 souls to every lineal mile. On Lake Mantumba there were sufficient people to allot 343 to every lineal mile. Along the Kwa River and Lake

Leopold II., after a careful estimate of the population, I find it able to furnish 100 men to every lineal mile of river-bank.

The traveller, after viewing the scantily peopled first and second regions, would scarcely be prepared for such a population. Indeed, he would have to ascend 100 miles above Stanley Pool before he would begin to feel assured that the population would approach even a respectable number. You must not suppose the people are scattered over the country with fields and gardens around their cottages, with here and there a steepled church; but along the Upper Congo the population is found grouped in long villages, ranging from a quarter of a mile to fifteen miles in length, separated by the primeval forest from each other; in the interior the villages cluster in the neighbourhood of the principal chief's village. They then are called districts, and between the outskirts of each district there may be six, ten, or twenty miles of uninhabited land left to nature, either covered by forest, or by thin bush, or by wild grass, wherein the game find secure shelter and subsistence.

To obtain a clear idea of the resources of Equatorial Africa let us consider this splendid stretch of navigable water on the main river between Stanley Pool and Stanley Falls. The distance is nearly 1100 miles, which will give us 2200 miles of river-banks separated by a stream which varies from a mile to sixteen miles in width. At least 700 miles of this length has an average breadth of four miles, which is divided into several channels by as many series of long and densely wooded islands.

Out of these 2200 miles of river-banks at

least 1500 miles are covered with thick woods, the islands are uninhabited, and the various channels of the river give access to 6000 miles of .island shores. Though the forests appear to be equal in height and thickness with any-thing similar seen in any tropical country, you must not imagine that every tree is valuable as building material. The carpenter and ship-wright would reject about a half of the trees as being too soft. The baobabs, cottonwoods, palms, and eschinomenae—though towering, massive, umbrageous, or beautiful in appear-ance, are altogether too fibrous and light for carpentry, nevertheless they have their uses. An ordinary baobab would furnish several tons of fibre, fit for rope, or paper; the eschinomenae would give good pith for solar topees; the cotton. woods furnish unsinkable canoes, and cotton for beds and pillows; the palms give wine, oil, and nutritious food for cattle. The creepers which run from one to the other in bewildering loops and festoons and knots, furnish the valuable caoutchouc, or consist of the useful rattan which we employ to seat chairs and sofas, or are used for walking-canes. The other half of the forest consists in almost equal quantities of good building timber, hard woods suitable for furniture and cabinet work, and those which are more useful for dyes, like the logwood of commerce, or produce valuable gum, for medicine, or for decorative purposes.

The soil underneath such primeval woods covers large deposits of fossil gum copal. Many of the grasses are available for rope and matting, for which the natives employ them extensively. The river, especially near grassy islets or grassy terraces, swarms with herds of hippo-

L

potami, and crocodiles infest every channel and creek. These Amphibia would furnish hides and ivory. Wild coffee and nutmegs are also found in certain portions of the forests on the main river. There is besides the rich product of the elephant. As we assume that there are 6000 miles of navigable water, we also assume that there must be 12,000 miles of river-banks, the inhabitants of which may be easily induced to hunt and trap the elephant for the sake of the ivory. For half a century yet to come this lately explored Congo basin will continue to supply many a score of tons of ivory annually to the European market.

Now the untutored natives will find no difficulty in supplying such raw products of the undeveloped Congo State to the pioneer traders. Within such an immense area, accessible to their steamers, the commercial pioneers ought to find abundant scope for their energies in skimming the mere cream of the trade. But the transport difficulties are so insuperable that even the cream of the Congo trade may not be indulged in. It must be remembered that every pound weight of produce costs about fivepence-halfpenny for carriage alone: thus—twopence three-farthings for the carriage of every pound weight of goods to purchase the African product, and twopence three-farthings for the carriage of the product itself to the European market. The African product must be of such value, then, as not only to pay such an expensive carriage, but also to pay for the heavy expenses of collection.

Except on a very large scale, it would not be prudent to trade in any article that would not sell for at least five times the cost of carriage, or say half-a-crown per lb. in a European market. Now of such raw African products, there are very few indeed that are worth such a price. Palm oil is worth only threepence per pound in Liverpool, kernels only about a penny farthing per pound, shelled ground-nuts about three-halfpence, and twenty other common trade articles vary from a penny to threepence per pound. The most valuable articles are indiarubber, which is worth from one shilling to two shillings per pound, coffee at threepence-halfpenny, cotton at fivepence-halfpenny, red gum copal at one shilling per pound, chillies fivepence-halfpenny, beeswax about a shilling, orchilla weed about fivepence, hippopotamus teeth two shillings, elephant tusks, which vary from four shillings and sixpence to ten shillings and sixpence per pound. By which you will perceive that a prudent trader would not venture to trade in any article but ivory, so long as the cost of carriage is so excessive. Yet, however abundant ivory may be, it cannot be so abundant that the trade in it will assure such a revenue to the State, as to render it self-supporting, or independent of the endowment fund given it by His Majesty King Leopold. For let us suppose that as many as 80 tons of ivory were annually exported from the State, the revenue from it would only amount to £3200 at £2 duty per cwt.

It will be thus seen that what would be beneficial for commerce would be equally so to the State. When freight is reduced from fivepence-halfpenny per pound to one penny per pound, then palm oil, camwood, coffee, cotton, gum copal, chillies, guinea grains, ginger, bees-

wax, orchilla weed, hippo teeth, and rubber may
be exported to Europe with profit.

To effect this reduction a light and cheap
railway must be constructed between the Lower
and the Upper Congo. Its construction would
expand commerce, by means of the river navigation, over the entire area of the Congo basin,
diffuse the blessings of civilisation and free
intercourse among many millions of Africans,
and be the means of consolidating the work of
King Leopold, and establishing upon a perma-
nent basis the State that he so munificently
endowed. Without the railway, as I have said so
often since I arrived in England in 1884, large
as its area may be, fertile and rich in natural
resources as the third region may be, the Congo
State is of as little use to the world at large, as it
can now be to the Government which administers
it, or to the generous monarch who founded it.

Last year I had great hopes that this railway—so necessary for the very existence and
consolidation of the State—was about to be
constructed. A body of men in this country
interested themselves—at the request of His
Majesty King Leopold—in the formation of a
syndicate for the construction of the Congo
Railway. Within a short time the syndicate was
formed, and a committee was appointed to proceed to Brussels to ascertain what concessions
the King was likely to grant. Within a week the
committee returned to England with a certain
number of concessions embodied in a signed
memorandum, which, though not remarkably
liberal compared to such as had been granted in
America and Australia, were still satisfactory to
the syndicate. The syndicate then set about
forming a company to obtain a charter, and

commence operations. By April of this year a draft charter was drawn out which contained in detail the concessions and privileges mentioned in the memorandum, and despatched to the Congo Government at Brussels. Since that month there have been held frequent meetings of the syndicate upon the various communications addressed to it by the Congo Government. The syndicate, out of its great respect for King Leopold, has endeavoured to meet the wishes of the gentlemen at Brussels, so far as it would be prudent for the success of the undertaking, but as several weeks have now elapsed since the last revised draft charter was sent to Brussels for approval, and no answer has been received, I am not free from certain misgivings that the railway will not be constructed so soon as I anticipated at the beginning of this year.

However, that is the position in which we are at present. It is entirely at the option of the State to sign the charter which will authorize the railway company to proceed with the enterprise, or to decline signing it, which will of course terminate all effort in this country in connection with it. You may well imagine then what a critical period the young State is in. It is either upon the point of initiating an enterprise which will end in creating the *sine qua non* of its very existence as a State, or of being compelled by its narrow means to contract itself within such limited territory as its Endowment Fund will enable it to govern usefully.

Here then I may properly end the lecture, which has been a summary of my Central African travels, from 1871 to June 1884,

and of the results which followed them,
viz. the recognition by Europe and the
United States of America of the territory
wherein we laboured the last few years as the
Congo Free State. With mutual goodwill the
Powers of the world have agreed to stand
aside, non-interfering, that the young State
might have an opportunity to grow and become
strong. On paper it exists a beautiful system of
polity and management—in fact a marvel of
politic art. It would be a thousand pities if the
practical government of it fell short of those
bright anticipations which I, in common with
all those who can admire the magnanimous
munificence and lofty philanthropy of the
Royal Founder, indulged in when the late
Berlin Conference ceased its labours.

Printed in the United States
By Bookmasters